Five Sextillion Atoms

Five Sextillion Atoms

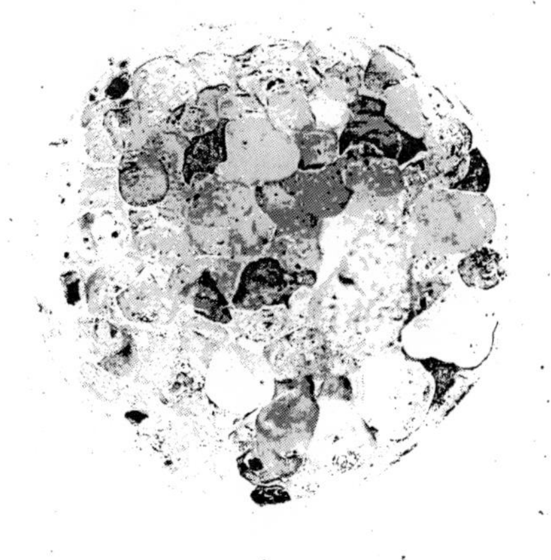

Jayne Benjulian

Saddle Road Press

Five Sextillion Atoms

Saddle Road Press
Hilo, Hawai'i
www.saddleroadpress.com

Author photograph by Marvin Kaplan
Cover and book design by Don Mitchell

ISBN 978-09969074-1-5
Library of Congress Control Number: 2015959347

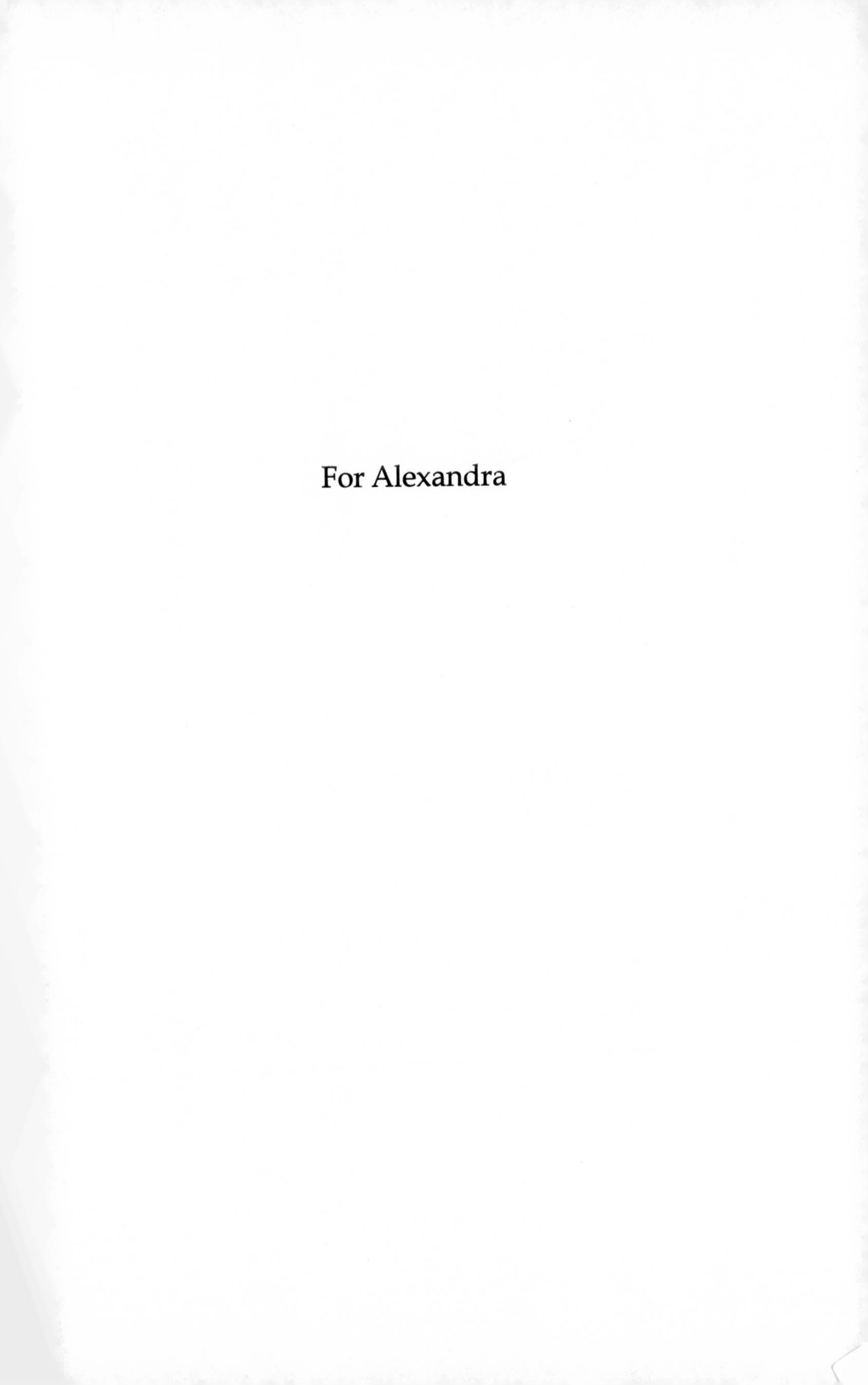

For Alexandra

Contents

Kaddish 13

Part One

Printemps 19
Jacinte 20
Garden 21
Ophelia 22
Elegy 23
August, Maine 24
Marine Incident 25
Lexington Avenue Line 26
Ode to Billy & Brenda 28
The infection 29
Clean 30

Part Two

Pistachios 35
Peace's Farm 37
Genesis 38
Banana Youth, 1968 39
Jill 41
Bim McSherry's name 42
Pearls 43
Wire 44
Nutmeg 45
Baby 46
Perseus 47
Julius 48
Concerning Bella 50
Ode to Steven 51
The Drop 52

Part Three

Pond	57
Vidalia	59
Ossabaw	61
Currents	62
Aubade	63
Site of *Klamath* Sinking	64
Quick	65
Winter	66
Three Winds	68
Enlightenment at Green Gulch	69
Timing	71
Notes	73
Acknowedgments	75
About Jayne Benjulian	77

Kaddish

In the attic deep enough for twenty
childhoods, an autograph book,
Oak School No. 3, resplendent in gold,
zipper teeth around pastel sheets,

Mother's signature shaky cursive.
Bundled in blankets, smaller than
a ten-year-old, fingers cold,
she felt awkward holding the pen.

A hurricane will blow tiles off the roof,
room will freeze, mouth open drinking rain.
You will always be, she wrote—
the rest will wash away.

Part One

Printemps

About to write
the dead live to twelve or twenty.

Have a black dress (bare arms) to wear
in the heat, a jacket, a hat,

red scarf from Printemps
to write about.

Jacinte

We walked through the cemetery,
William Cognat's grave blasted

by an oak, cement chunks
shoved up hillsides,

Cognat tossed to one side,
his wife to another,

huge trunk breaking
whatever was left to break.

I want a tree to grow through me.
That's how Jacinte spoke.

Ship my ashes to Thailand—
the children will have to travel.

In the spring we flew to Chiang Mai,
threw her into the river;

I returned to the Strait
of Juan de Fuca

to lie and to wait.

Garden

On a breeze,
the angel balances.

No one remembers
her words exactly,

a tone, white piano keys
in the high range,

a bow soothing its violin.
Gate locked:

when we look in,
starlight on stone.

Ophelia

Had he been a woman, Hamlet would wonder:
to feel or not to feel, whether to walk
ramparts in the dead of night,
is it safe. His mother would be his father,
married ere funeral meats were cold,
none would he eat in our great hall
(but in private devour all). Your mother's
sister not your father's brother, your lover,
your best friend—What is your weapon?
Pressure diverts the ache, like sweet
when the mouth burns, like snow
when bone breaks. Can you play the scene?
Invisible your watery exit, I'd have
liked to see you queened.

ELEGY

Gorgeous fruit,
then weeds,
then middle age
to which you devoted,
of all things, poetry,

honest words
about lies:
Yellow farm house,
site of our decay.

But I remember
moon-fields,
deer bending in fog.

Last sweet taste.

August, Maine

Next to the barbeque, dark
folded trees blue,

his daughter near the pond,
imagining, stream turning up

its volume. Everywhere under
us, rocks, farmers cursing rocks

in their fields. Bats are back,
a good thing, yadda yadda,

bats who can zoom into your hair,
impossible to extract.

Against the screen, black wings
beat, I slam the window down

and trap it in that cell,
bloody murder, summer closing in,

blood on the trunk room floor, those
who said they'd set it free, liars all.

Marine Incident

Waves in the wake, stern

        heaves into piling,

Mother in life jacket opens her mouth,
white arms flapping like flags before

a storm, Father in his captain's cap
picks up the ship-to-shore

their legs quick-quick-slow.

        We are on the flying bridge:

we look down on them in blue air,

        Father, Mother in clouds of orange pillow,

bow rocking,

        she has been away, now

returned, the terror shocked
out of her—

        she slips rail to rail

as if dancing.

Lexington Avenue Line

We are sneaking you in, my sister tells me.
I am supposed to feel special,

but the occasion mystifies.
In the room, edges,

blankets, sheets,
underneath, curve of Mother's body.

She is ninety pounds,
my father whispers behind me

at her hospital bed,
a train and subway ride away from home.

We descend, outside,
descend again,

I am under earth, I hesitate, doors slam,
two steel monoliths that could crush me.

He doesn't tell me to say goodbye,
so when he is ingesting more morphine

than food, I say, *Will you dream of me?*
Yes, he smiles. But Mother

is silent, he is silent.
Before is fuzzy. After is fuzzy.

Doors are sharp.

Ode to Billy & Brenda

The morning we polished their beaks & dropped
them in the duck pond, they followed us back
to the parking lot quacking as we peeled
away. Next Saturday, no carmine beaks.

Does pond water eradicate nail polish?
Or did our ducks fail to acclimate?
Oh, we had our last rites—toy chest coffin,
steel camp trunk circa 1965

topped with 2,4,5-T-infused farm dirt—
but biters we marked & then abandoned,
Billy, named after the neighbor who kissed

my sister in the cow barn, Corona Park
World's Fair, Brenda, after nurse
who painted Mother's nails & clipped her hair.

The infection

came from red ants—they built their nests
in roots of blighted madrone
which kowtowed to the oak.

She hung from that oak, named it Sylvie—
her own name *smart aleck*—
hung from her knees,

succored ants with Good n' Plenty,
raisinets, pistachio shells
while the question raged like a fever:

how to become a she?
Furry sweaters, cleavage, no scratching
(scabs, butt, sticky mascara, ankles

ants ate like manna
plummeting onto their turf
when she dropped to earth).

Clean

What was the word I can't remember,
what words did I know at nine?
Plenty with a father like mine. His sister
cornered me. Was it the stone
room, it had a porch door
a stranger could come in, was Mother
alive I can't remember who slept
upstairs, I turned the knob to the attic
door, it was cold, it was hot, I looked
through the box, smelled her cashmere clothes,
bra with a plastic straw attached,
blew air in the cup, slipped into the straps—
was it a curse word or a bad thought? Don't say.

Part Two

Pistachios

The day the clocks move forward
she considers which hour she would like to lose,

the hour chased through pantry,
dining room, den with a knife in her pants

to hurt Father's giant hand
when he spanks her for eating the pistachios.

Which hour out of more than twenty-four?

Hour in the Sylvie tree,
Father at his pen factory,

brother at Scouts, wind
troubling leaves in the yard.

Hour in the blue room's corner

Father whispers a thing to Mother,
back to the hospital,

I knew it, the girl shrieks (triumphant
to know a secret)—

it is then he turns on her his iron wings,
yanks their secret from the room,

when her own curls are grey,
her mother's curls will still be black,

and it will still be spring.

Peace's Farm

Her father owns the factory—he can talk on the phone
whenever he wants, but he doesn't want. She tries to keep
him talking until her mother comes home. Probably there
are errands. She never returns until the boy is finished with
his Scout meeting. Elvis the cat jumps down from the sink.

Three houses down, Frances Schechter beeps twice and
rolls her Caddy into the driveway. Night is black as ice,
as the crack of it falling. Inside her knee, knee a bone saw
will slice in one billion eight hundred seconds, spider spins
close. No one comes to the river she thinks she made up the
name for: Nile. No one has told her this name existed before
history, a shock to read her word on a map at school.

Moist air chills window glass now, dirt that was Peace's
Farm, where the farmer planted and sprayed, and corn grew
as tall as swings she pumps so high, her mother looking up
from her lilies, waving her brown arms.

Genesis

I stand on the shore of Long Island Sound,
east, my parents say, you can see Europe.

Somewhere between Madrid and Barcelona,
my tongue touched Castilian *c*,

French *r* has to do with air
slipped behind a glottal stop

not quite stopped.

Russian consonants crash—
                                        zdraftsvicha, *dacha*—

like continents,
time lifts at fault lines,

splits the earth we knew,
impassible: walk through.

Banana Youth, 1968

When the committee named
Father to a post
in a foreign consulate,
Mother said:

A shanda from the Yidden?
Don't you dare.

The day I found out I was one,
I knew I was doomed,
like the conceited, unpleasant
Rutka in my class.

In the square, our politzia
clubbed us,
thud in the center of my back.

We renounced our passports.
The government invented
a document.
My teacher said:
it's best.

20,000 zlotys
for my schooling.
Every Wednesday a train
came: Sweden, Denmark,
Vienna.

We spoke like Poles.

At the station, she gave
me lilies. This was not
expulsion—they called it
an invitation to leave.

Jill

She was—the way a girl
could be—a friend, without

knowing much. We were
in the classroom closet,

its multiple doors sheltering
lunch boxes, kazoos, maps,

Encyclopedia Britannica,
one door open, down its length

a ten-foot human skeleton unfurled.
Jill—who was she?—

That's your mother, she spat.

Bim McSherry's name

belongs to a small boy
who comes and goes
to and from a doll house,
the kind people actually fit
in, store bicycles in,
or in back of, play doctor.
He touches someone's skin.
Her name more ordinary.
Time will change how he sees,
how he is seen,
what he remembers:
windows without glass—
rain raining in.

Pearls

The odd thing is, my brother is missing.
We lock arms in a semi-circle: cousins
and friends, girls in their padded bras.
Where am I? he asks.

December, six months since our father
became our sole parent. My father
is going steady—he doesn't tell us
he is already married. He and his date

light a candle for the bar mitzvah boy.
Rhinestones around her wrist,
she twists with cousin Dick.

But outside, the boy catches snowflakes
on his eyelids, someone bends to kiss his face,
her pearl earrings against his cheek.

Wire

1

I left him once
when he disappeared for a day
I left him once
no one heard a word—he surfaced
later—what did he imagine—
time froze when he stepped off the earth.
I left him once.

2

Then I asked him:
what rose up and what descended,
then I asked him
the definition of honor,
lie of omission, who are you
person with whom I am speaking?
Then I asked him.

3

But it was not
the beginning, the beginning—
but it was not
all there was. There was a child's
voice soldered to our veins, chill
and burning current—say his name—
but he did not.

Nutmeg

In her story about Nutmeg, her father
buys the dog. I am not there, do not find
the ad, make the call, drive to the kennel,
kneel down to let the puppy lick my hands.
He buys the red sneakers, which is why they
cannot be thrown out. *I bought them*, I say.
We came to this store a year ago. No,
she says, *Daddy bought them in Chicago.*
But he hasn't lived in Chicago for years,
I say. This is how things go: for two more
months she will not see him. Tonight she says
her body hurts. She tucks her head against
my lips so I can feel. Somewhere he lights
a match, but here is where she burns.

Baby

I find him on the beach
stone eye full of sand
his body smooth as years
trunk and legs tucked tight—

ocean-going trauma
leaving home—
just a baby really.
I close my palms around him,

touch his bones with my nose
the way elephants do,
he is stone, I know, but

pretend I'm his mother
fallen on her knees,
cover him with leaves.

Perseus

And here is Perseus. Kidneys
don't pump, every morning poked
with intravenous fluids,
one day, he refuses.

All afternoon, he whines until I lock
him in the blueberry patch. Late at night,
he butts his head against mine,
winds himself in my hair.

Bump him over, he caresses.
I hold the line. Sometime before morning,
he slips out. Showers of gold
rain down, my enemies turn to stone.

Julius

After my father died and all his money
went to his wife, I held out hope we'd receive
a gift, paltry sum that spoke affection from the grave—

but nothing. She gave the money to her sons
the weaker one admitted when I faced him down.
Did I want to say something? A eulogy?

It didn't seem like such a great idea at the time,
but for the record I shall compose it here:
A Flawed Man, who could walk out of Lee Shore's studio

never collect my brother's bar mitzvah album
because he argued with the photographer
about the price. The stepmother's name? Rita.

After the funeral, I found a marriage certificate
dated six months before the wedding.
An ultimatum, marry me now or it's off.

That's the guy alright. Old mink coats,
a piano—my piano—disappeared.
You were in California, she said.

My own brother wouldn't talk to me.
I had lived with them, I was the enemy.
On the path from San Anselmo to Terra Linda,

a woman with two German shepherds,
both four years old, one all muscle, ears
at attention that German shepherd way,

the other puppy-sized. He walked
in circles. Brain damaged, she said,
attacked, while trying to eat food

put down by a kennel boy who,
leaving, left the pups locked in
with a mother not their own.

Concerning Bella

Gravitas, the manager said,
flipping résumé pages,

he stared at the demilitarized
zone on my head from roots to ear,

white advancing south from the crown,
chestnut retreating down. He

should have known Bella, my
Romanian grandmother, she

sold pencils to the army, ran
her sons like a combat unit, chopped

liver like a samurai,
her white coils vibrating like a power

grid around her eggplant cheeks.
Zoftig: from *zaft*, juice, sap—

she had gravitas.

Bella, Bella, Bella,

before I knew it meant beauty,
it sounded like combat to me.

Ode to Steven

My stepbrother pretended to hypnotize me,
I pretended enchantment. In this way
we touched. Each year his mother reminded
me, *today is the anniversary*
of his death, don't you forget.
Ah, Rita, I cannot forget the year,
abandoned Hobbits on the shelf, the CNN
pundit who was his high school friend.
Dear, she wrote, *could have, will never, himself.*
On-screen, lines disappear from her face,
her auburn hair comes back to life,
her opinion counts: Snowden, exiled
to a foreign country, exposed our ills.
Stepbrother, hotel with pills.

The Drop

Compare him to what he once was,
lucid, voluptuous. Can we say that

of a father? His chin, even
his nose droops, triceps flap.

A drop from a pine tree
graphs its weight against the pane,

pines lift from each other,
and sharpen air he breathes—

windows open even in winter,
especially in winter—the drop

gives its weight to the pane,
abandons itself, what little's left,

oh gravity, mid-pane,

it has no body left to drag,
single axis, graph of the heart,

old self, five sextillion atoms.

Part Three

Pond

On a rise between two cedars
a blue sedan leans into silt,

window zipped tight
and tinted—

inside a lovers' secret
we will not unwind—

considers whether it might tilt
into the slide or right itself.

Branches net the sky,
swamp.

He moves forward.
His chances are slim—

he doesn't swim, it's dark, his heart.

Bubble by bubble
blue metal sinks down.

Now door handle,
now frogs or is it toads,

a siren on the road.

He dared
or wished to dare

and slipped this silver night
around my shoulders.

Vidalia

They're everywhere and priced
like gourmet items, but when I first

ate them, no one had ever heard
of an onion with the name of a town.

In Vidalia, timber barons were kings,
their wives ordered Christmas

gifts from Neiman Marcus,
folks knew Georgia towns

if they had been there:

Valdosta,
girls' basketball champions,

Ossabaw,
crabs gave themselves

for a string and cheap bait,
and I could ride the Crescent

from Atlanta to New Orleans,
houses levitating

above Pontchartrain,
time as thin as onion skin:

woods, winter morning,
dog's footfall, beat, beat,

beat of her herding paws,
another Christmas, new boots

from Gokey, my own .22,
silent, air

shot with surrender,
quail,

quail in the hands
of those long-legged men.

Ossabaw

Leaving the mainland, we shed watches,
wallets, phones, clocks & boarded the skiff
for Ossabaw, where the painter & I,
on a live oak log, cracked oysters: split
hinges, gulped down lump after shining lump
until our blood-lemon fingers ached,
tide swept our hors d'oeuvres out to sea
& a wild hog absconded with my backpack
(five days later, recovered in mud,
straps & zipper more or less intact).
In one city or another, I lost
his painting of cypress shadow on the tidal
creek, but my forest-stained pack—
dusk inside it—that I kept.

Currents

A black bird rides a wave
between tide and man—
or is it a tall boy?
Odd for a bird to swell so near.

The sun draws down,
boy's white hat, burning maple,
not a bird but a plane
he commands.

What might you have been,
wings of a boy,
boy with wings,
sand, sand,

return, return,
vortex of eddies,
frigid air,
sea smoke.

Aubade

When light struck, I found the dog
next to me, head on your pillow,
shape mimicking your curve
before you turned toward serious sleep.
Heat seemed abstract, something
I didn't have to face until
inhabiting a city with no ocean,
all day I lived indoors.
You left your physics books, a desk,
in all those hollow spaces
fossils baking: arrowhead,
petrified fish embracing.
(Morning sounds
like what it means.)

Site of *Klamath* Sinking

A post marks the trail above
the wreck. Twenty-four sailors

returning to the mill, hold empty,
ship bashed against cove.

They tumbled, choked on salt.
Cliff smelled like clove.

Here I threw my gold
band into the Pacific.

A decade later, I found the site
flowered with Indian Paintbrush

flaming against its own green arms.

Quick

1

Here lies Father
his still black hair at 86.
Here lies Father
turned to the corner staring at
my knitting needles, click clack, crack
a blanket for baby's nap.

2

Any time now,
sweet, you will run to me, exclaim
you've hurt your bloody, bloody knee,
make it better, clean it, kiss it
come, before (any time now) I
forget your name.

Winter

We have left you certain things
in a safety deposit box:
diamond earrings, birth records,

letter on pink stationery.
From the back seat of a taxi,
I watched you knock on the screen door,

disappear into a pair of arms.
These are your parents.
You have his bean-pole shape

(they were gangly teenagers, too).
For me, it was two hours in the liquor store
or Dunkin' Donuts. Outside, stop lights

green, yellow, endless returning.
I held on to one poor cup of coffee.
You emerged clutching a blood-red

rose. A blizzard of turnstiles—
nothing could persuade you
to let that flower go until

weary running for the last train,
you released it to me.
A thousand petals floated to the floor.

In that volcanic silence of the ruined rose,
I stole you from them.
One single day I allow you to ascend.

Three Winds

Would Mother be young, standing in the middle
of Knight Street talking to Frances Druck?
Hem of her yellow apron ripples.
She looks back at the quiet house, spot
where a child's mouth fogs a circle
on the living room window. Did she say
take care of the children, sentence blurred
to dust, like grey on a neglected table
caretaker blows away. Atomized
in three directions. Call her back.
Once, she appeared in silk of memory
waiting for our lives to begin. In the moment
my heart locks, I try a key, turning;
turning a tunnel at the end of our lives.

Enlightenment at Green Gulch

A poor workman blames his tools,

I heard him say three thousand times
between the age of five and eighteen.

I put miles between us,
drove west to hear some peaceful

sound slip from my own throat,
build a nest and sing in it.

Green Gulch Farm, residents
tolerate visitors,

a priest stops sweeping to scold me,
I've come too close to his teahouse.

In the meditation garden,
Buddha's in his own shed,

eyelids lowered toward his floor,
he has found what I am searching for.

Pay attention to the path.
Marigolds and pansies, crowns

and robes, what gift in the light grove?
Lichen-covered bench with a plaque:

Jennifer Gordon
born May 27, 1965
missing October 18, 1994

Be careful what you wish for,
but I was halfway out the door.

Timing

for J.S.

Under the tray in my desk drawer
I found your letter in its envelope,

written when you were my age.

It is hospital white.

Your book is done, your wife has lupus.

Send your poems out, you say.

One of your fingers, one that read pulses,
lifted the hair behind my ear,

sealed the note.

How tidy the line I held.

Doctor, poet,

now we should meet.

Notes

"Banana Youth," a translation from the Polish phrase, was used as an epithet for the children of communist bureaucrats, many of them Jews, who had money to buy fruit. Between 1968 and 1969, about twenty thousand to twenty-five thousand Jews left Poland. The borders were open for Jews—but not for Poles—so that Jews might emigrate to Israel, the beneficiary, pro-government newspapers suggested, of Jewish spy rings and shipments of gold. "Banana Youth" is for Krysia and Basia.

"Currents" is dedicated to Heather McHugh, who saw "vortex of eddies" and "sea smoke" in the waters of Maine.

Acknowedgments

For sharp, generous responses to this manuscript I am grateful to the Warren Wilson Program for Writers, especially Mary Leader and Martha Rhodes; to Marianne Boruch, Maurice Manning, Debra Allbery, and Ellen Bryant Voigt, who set the bar high; and to Heather McHugh, my first, last, and most exacting reader. Thank you to David Wojahn for rich suggestions about revision.

Thank you to colleagues and friends, named and unnamed; to Sandra Hunter, Marcia Meier, Tania Pryputniewicz, Lisa Rizzo, Barbara Rockman, Michelle Wing, and Barbara Ann Yoder for their support and wisdom; Michael Collins; and the formidable Wild Bloomers: Nancy Allen, Carla Lowe Baku, Alexandra Carter, Allen Chamberlain, Lynette D'Amico, Patricia Grace King, Ellen McCulloch-Lovell, Adrienne Perry, and Judith Whelchel. To audiences who listened to versions of these poems at readings and to Peg Alford Pursell, the brilliant curator of Why There Are Words, thank you. I am lucky to have worked with Ruth Thompson and Don Mitchell at Saddle Road Press and Marvin Kaplan, photographer. To Bill I say, love has meant everything.

I wish to thank the editors of the publications in which these poems, sometimes in slightly different form, first appeared:

Agni: "Vidalia"
Barrow Street: "Printemps"
Café Review: "Three Winds" and "Wire"
Cider Press Review: "Clean"
Cimarron Review: "Nutmeg"
The Ilanot Review: "Kaddish" and "Peace's Farm"
Mother Writer Mentor: "Winter"
Nimrod International: "Timing"
Rappahannock Review: "Jacinte"
Spillway: "Lexington Avenue Line" and "Genesis"
Women's Review of Books: "Jill" and "Pearls"
Writing Fire (Green River Press, 2015): "Concerning Bella"

"Lexington Avenue Line" also appeared in *Poetry Daily.*

About Jayne Benjulian

Jayne Benjulian has always been a writer. She grew up in suburban backyards near New York City and spent summers swimming in the Atlantic Ocean. Drawn to coastlines, she also lived on the West Coast—on an island, in a cabin in the hills, and a house under the redwoods. She began writing as a young girl, leaving letters under the mattress to read years later and see who she had been. Her work appears in numerous journals including, *Agni*, *Barrow Street*, *Poet Lore*, *Ms.*, *Nimrod International*, *Women's Review of Books* and *Poetry Daily*.

Jayne's careers have been as varied and many as places she has lived: she served as chief speechwriter at Apple, investigator for the public defender in King County, Washington, and director of new play development at Magic Theater. She was an Ossabaw Island Project Fellow; a teaching fellow at Emory University, where she earned an MA; a lecturer in the Graduate Program in Theater at San Francisco State University; and a Fulbright Teaching Fellow in Lyon, France.

She holds an MFA from the Warren Wilson Program for Writers. She lives in Massachusetts and hikes the Berkshire Hills with her long-haired German shepherd, Ophelia, but she misses her big, brash Pacific Ocean. *Five Sextillion Atoms* is her first collection.

Find out more about Jayne and her work at www.jaynebenjulian.com.

CPSIA information can be obtained at www.ICGtesting.com
Printed in the USA
LVOW07s1711280916

506567LV00004B/860/P